CW00959399

An Introduction to

Medieval Enamels

COVER ILLUSTRATION

Case for a small book or relic, English or French, mid-14th century.
Silver-gilt with translucent enamels.
Depicting scenes from a romance, probably that of Sir Enyas and the wodewose (wildman): front, a mounted knight is fighting a wodewose armed with a club and shield; back, another knight is giving his spear to a lady leaning from castle battlements. The same romance is shown in contemporary manuscripts such as *British Library Yates Thompson 13*.
Secular subjects are uncommon on medieval enamels.
h. 5.6 cm., w. 5.0 cm., d. 2.0 cm.
218-1874

1

Spoon detail, Netherlandish, mid-15th century.
Painted enamel on silver, inlaid on the handle with niello.
The scene on the bowl is very like a series on the Monkey Cup in the Metropolitan Museum, New York, and both may derive from a lost romance. Amongst luxurious domestic items from the same workshop is a spoon in the Boston Fine Art Museum, USA showing a fox preaching to geese.
l. 24.1 cm.
C.2-1935

An Introduction to

Medieval Enamels

Marian Campbell

Department of Metalwork
Victoria and Albert Museum

LONDON: HER MAJESTY'S STATIONERY OFFICE

First published 1983

Series editor Julian Berry
Designed by HMSO/Graphic Design
Printed in the UK for HMSO

ISBN 0 11 290385 1
Dd 696422 C65

To the memory of H. P. Mitchell Keeper of the Department of Metalwork 1923-6

Acknowledgements: I should like to thank the following who have helped me with this book—Claude Blair, Graham Brandon, Alan Dingle, Peter Macdonald and Nigel Morgan.

Photocredits: 19b London Society of Antiquaries, 22 National Gallery of Art, Washington, 36 Robert Braunmüller, Munich.

HER MAJESTY'S STATIONERY OFFICE

Government Bookshops

49 High Holborn, London WC1V 6HB
13a Castle Street, Edinburgh EH2 3AR
Brazennose Street, Manchester M60 8AS
Southey House, Wine Street, Bristol BS1 2BQ
258 Broad Street, Birmingham B1 2HE
80 Chichester Street, Belfast BT1 4JY

Government Publications are also available through booksellers

The full range of Museum publications is displayed and sold at
The Victoria & Albert Museum, South Kensington, London SW7 2RL

Introduction

The brilliant jewel-like colours of enamel have ensured it a prestige that has lasted for at least 3000 years. The technique of fusing coloured glass to a metal surface by intense heat has been used for centuries to embellish the most highly prized objects, from the altarpieces and reliquaries of the Church to the crowns and drinking cups of kings. The V&A has an outstanding collection of pre-Renaissance enamels, that range in date from the Iron Age to the fifteenth century, and in place of origin from Ireland to Constantinople.

Only the very wealthy could afford enamels, for, despite the negligible intrinsic value of glass, enamelwork commanded immense prices. No doubt this was partly a recognition of the considerable technical skill required to transform glass into enamel, and partly a response to its spectacular appearance. It is easy for us to underestimate medieval man's appetite for colour, when time, restoration, and Reformation have muted the original effect of his ecclesiastical interiors, once resplendent with wall-paintings, stained glass and polychrome statuary.

Enamels significantly extended the expressive range of the metalworker's craft. Whereas the other decorative techniques at his command—the use of gems, engraving and embossing—produced merely patterns in colour or monochrome pictures, with enamel the craftsman could create an enduring polychrome image and tell a story as forcefully as any painter.

A great range of items were adorned with enamels during the medieval period, so that the most useful approach to a history of the subject is not to generalise about classes of objects, but rather to describe the rise and fall in popularity of the various techniques of enamelling: cloisonné, champlevé, translucent, and their lesser variants. However, any such account must be a piecemeal and uncertain chronicle. Enamels, being portable, fragile and precious have always been particularly vulnerable to the vagaries of fortune—theft, damage, and the melting pot—so that surviving examples cannot be considered as wholly representative. This may distort our picture of medieval enamels, as may the particular bias of the V&A collection, but to rectify the latter I shall mention examples that are held by other institutions.

Technique

The word enamel derives, via the Old French *esmail*, from the Old High German *smelzen*, to smelt—the process most crucial to the making of enamel. To prepare enamel the constituents of glass, flint or sand, red lead and soda or potash are heated together to form a clear flux, to which is added, as a colouring agent, a metallic oxide—copper for green, cobalt for blue, iron for red or brown. The enamel is then allowed to cool and solidify in slabs. Before use, each colour is separately ground into a fine powder and washed to remove any dirt. The powder is then placed on the prepared metal surface, allowed to dry, and fired in an enclosed kiln at a temperature of between 700° and 800°C. Successive firings usually have to be used to build up a greater thickness of enamel, and a wider range of colours. When cool, the surface is polished to remove imperfections and add brilliance to the colours.

The difference between the various enamelling techniques lies chiefly in the methods used to prepare the metal surface for the enamel, methods that are to a great extent governed by the physical properties of that particular metal.

Cloisonné (cell-work)—thin strips of metal are bent to form the outline of a design and are soldered edge-on to the surface of the metal object. The resulting cells are then filled with enamel, often restricted to one colour per cell. Because of the delicacy of such work, soft metals such as gold or silver are most suitable.Gold cloisonné was commonest on small items, such as jewellery, but larger base metal surfaces were often decorated with a series of separately applied gold cloisonné plaques [plates 3,4,5,6,7,8,9].

Plique-à-jour—a form of cloisonné in which the backing for the metal strips is removed after firing, leaving a network of cells filled with enamel; since the enamel is translucent this produces the effect of a stained glass window [plate 36].

Filigree—a variation of cloisonné in which filigree wire takes the place of the metal strips.

Champlevé—in a way, the reverse of the cloisonné technique; the design is gouged out of the surface of the metal (rather like a lino-cut) leaving thin ridges of metal standing above the resulting troughs and channels. Enamel is then placed in the depressions. Often several colours may be included in a single compartment. The process requires a substantial thickness of metal, and was therefore used on base metals such as copper or bronze, whose relative cheapness allowed much larger objects to be made than did gold and silver [plates 2a,c,e,f, 10-24, 27, 28].

Basse-taille (translucent enamel)—a development of the champlevé technique. Its chief characteristic is that translucent enamel is used on a base of gold or silver, onto which a design in low relief has been chased or engraved. Great tonal richness and subtlety in the modelling of forms can be achieved by variations in the depth of the engraving and hence the thickness of the enamel, through which light is reflected back from the metal base [plates 25,26,29-33].

Niello—a black metal alloy of silver, sulphur and lead. It was often used to achieve the same effect as champlevé enamel.

Email en ronde bosse (encrusted enamel)—the technique of enamelling the irregular surface of figures, or of objects, in the round or in very high relief. These small-scale sculptural compositions are invariably of gold or silver, whose surface is roughened to hold the enamel coating in place.

Painted enamel—this technique is fundamentally different from the others, in that the various colours are not separated from each other by metal ridges of any sort, and the metal ground itself requires no special preparation; the skills required, in fact, are less those of a goldsmith than of a painter. The metal normally used was copper and, very occasionally, gold or silver [plates 1 & 38].

Early History

The history of the discovery and early use of enamelling is obscure, but the technique seems to have been invented independently in a number of widely separated places. Any craftsman with a competence in both glassworking and metalworking might have seen the decorative potential of combining the two media: a metal surface brilliantly and permanently coloured in such a way as to simulate precious stones. The history of enamelling in the Middle Ages shows the use of a number of different means to this end, of metals and techniques that rose and fell in popularity.

Although the Ancient Egyptians made jewellery decorated with coloured glass cut and laid into cells, there is as yet no evidence that they practised the closely-related process of enamelling. Its first users were probably the Myceneans, who were highly skilled metalworkers. The earliest known examples of enamelling occur on Mycenean jewellery of about 1450 BC: gold beads decorated with blobs of dark blue enamel set in hollows surrounded by more tiny gold beads. The first known cloisonné enamelling appears on a gold sceptre of 1200-1100 BC discovered in Cyprus and now in the Cyprus Museum. The terminal of the sceptre consists of two naturalistic hawks set with cells that contain green, white and mauve opaque enamel; it is uncertain whether the craftsmen were of Mycenean, Cypriot or Egyptian origin. From this may have evolved the filigree enamel which appears first on a gold Assyrian diadem of the seventh century BC, decorated by rosettes with enamel petals. From the sixth century BC Greek goldsmiths, working as far afield as Russia and Etruria, regularly employed filigree enamel on jewellery.

The Romans apparently used enamel sparingly, although some glass jewellery of the first century AD survives, in which the glass is inlaid with gold cell-work which in turn contains enamel. However, at the northern fringes of the Roman Empire the native tribes seem, by the third century BC, to have been using red enamel on bronze to simulate coral inlay. Champlevé enamel on bronze was particularly common on brooches, ornamental horse-harness and on the medallions used to decorate hanging-bowls. The earliest known historical mention of enamelling may well refer to this

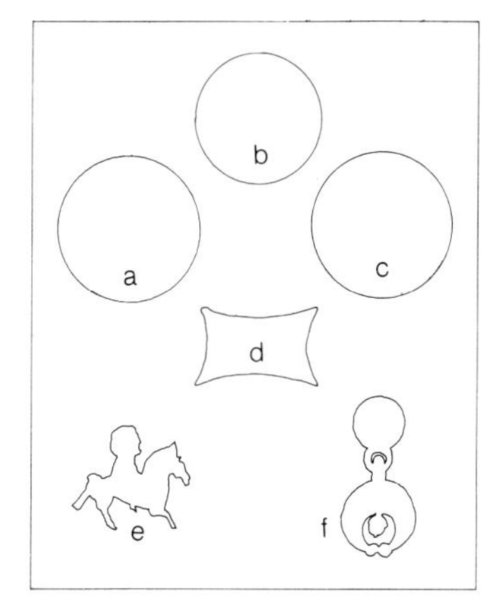

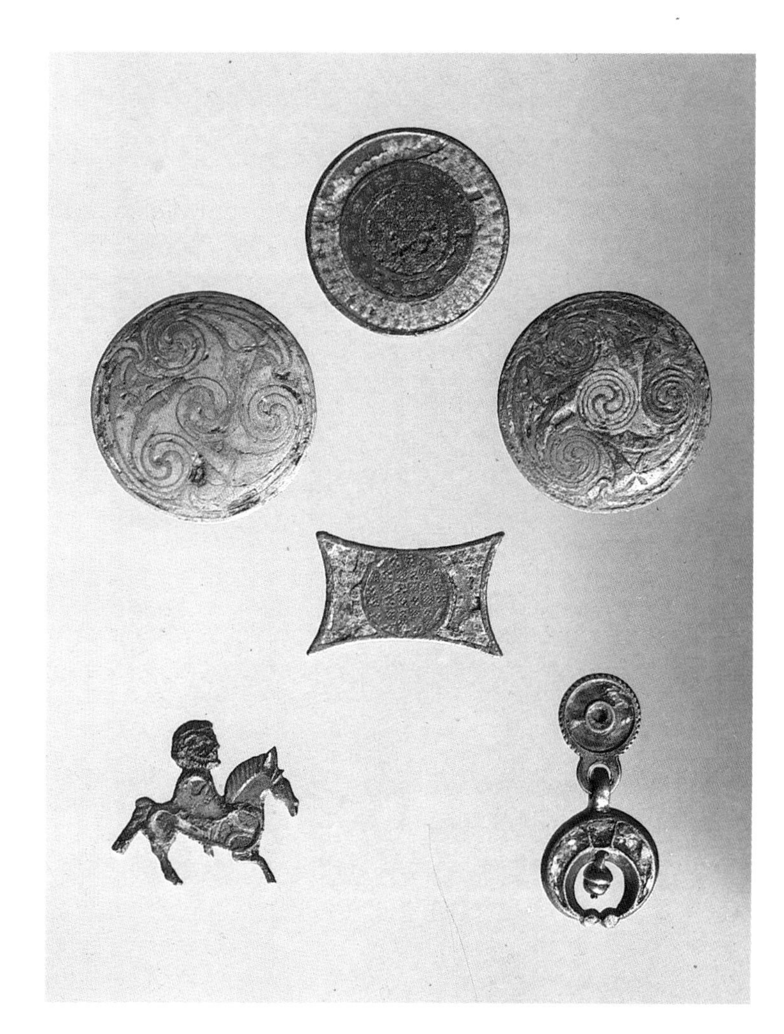

2
Celtic enamels.

a & c
Ornamental escutcheons, British, 6-7th century.
Champlevé enamel on bronze.
Probably from hanging bowls which were suspended from chains and are thought to have been used for ritual purposes. Several have been excavated in the British Isles; one of the most famous forms part of the 7th century Sutton Hoo hoard in the British Museum. C was dug up near Hitchin, Herts.
a) dia. 4.8 cm. c) dia. 4.6 cm.
6926-1860 M.163-1923

b & d
Studs, Romano-Celtic, 1-2nd century.
Bronze with millefiori enamel.
Probably dress fastenings or horse trappings. D was found near Eden Hall, Cumberland, with Roman coins of 117-161 AD.
b) dia. 4.3 cm. d) w. 4 cm. h. 2.7 cm.
4098-1857 4898-1901

e
Horse and rider brooch, Romano-Celtic, 2-3rd century.
Bronze with champlevé enamel.
Found in 1838 at Kirkby Thore with Roman coins of 69-235 AD.
l. 4.1 cm.
4893-1901

f
Ornament from horse harness, Romano-Celtic, 2-3rd century.
Bronze with champlevé enamel.
Dug up near Hatherop, Glos.
w. 2.4 cm. h. 5 cm.
M.16-1920

provincial work. Philostratus, a Greek philosopher of the second century AD, describes a boar hunt at which the riders have brightly coloured horse-trappings:

> It is said that the barbarians in the Ocean pour these colours on heated bronze and that they adhere, become hard as stone and preserve the designs that are made on them. (*Icones*, Lib.I, 28)

The earliest enamels in the V&A are of Romano-Celtic origin; medallions in which champlevé enamel relieves the pattern of trumpet-shaped spirals characteristic of much Celtic art [plate 2 a & c]. Other items are decorated with *millefiori*—bundles of thin glass rods of various colours and shapes fused together, drawn out, cut into slices and then fused on to a ground of coloured enamel, a process perhaps derived from Roman glass-making practices.

Enamelled jewellery, especially brooches in the shape of animals or crossbows, survives in some quantity from Northern Europe. A large enamel jewellery workshop of the mid-third century has been excavated at Anthée in Belgium, but such jewellery was undoubtedly made over a wide area, including the British Isles. Larger items, such as cups, jars and wine-ladles, were also enamelled: in the V&A there is the foot of a cup or bowl, and in the British Museum the second-century 'Battersea Shield', made of beaten bronze and decorated with red and blue enamel roundels. Enamels of this type probably went on being produced in the British Isles, Gaul, Bohemia and southern Germany until at least as late as the seventh century.

Byzantine Enamels

Byzantine enamels probably derive from classical Greek antecedents. They consist most commonly of cloisonné enamel on a precious metal, usually gold, and seem to have been used mainly on items of liturgical or ceremonial significance, and on jewellery.

Enamels which predate the Iconoclast controversy (726-842), when many images connected with the Church were destroyed, are exceptionally rare. The earliest probably dates from the late fifth or early sixth century: such as the gold medallion, with a bust of the Empress Eudoxia surrounded by a cloisonné laurel-wreath, in the Cabinet des Medailles, Paris. Further rare survivals are the late sixth or early seventh century gold pectoral cross embellished with enamelled birds now in Dumbarton Oaks, Washington, and the silver and enamel Fieschi-Morgan reliquary of the True Cross in the Metropolitan Museum, New York.

The greatest period of Byzantine enamelling was from the ninth to the twelfth century. The treasury of St Mark's, Venice, has an abundance of pieces from this era, notably the votive crown thought to depict the Emperor Leo VI (886-912) which is one of the few such enamels which can be approximately dated.

From the tenth century onwards, Byzantine fashion seems to have favoured enamelled figures against a background of unadorned metal rather than the wholly enamelled surfaces of the earlier period. The most splendid example of this is Limburg Cathedral's reliquary of the True Cross, which, according to its inscription, was made for Basil, illegitimate son of the Emperor Romanos I Licapenos (920-48).

The V &A's plaque of a dancing girl [plate 4] closely resembles a series, now in the National Museum, Budapest, from the crown of the Emperor Constantine IX Monomachos (1042-55). Doubts have been cast on its authenticity, but, assuming it to be genuine, certain technical differences suggest that it is either a slightly later replacement plaque from the Emperor's crown, or part of another, similar series, made for the crown of the Emperor's consort.

The masterpiece of the later Byzantine period is the 'Pala d'Oro', the golden altarpiece of St Mark's, Venice, which is both the largest extant monument to the Byzantine enameller's art and one of the most problematic. Its 137 enamels reveal a mixture of style and period. Records state that the *Pala* was first erected in 1105, renewed in 1209 and finally remodelled in 1345. Of its enamels, which are mostly of the eleventh and twelfth century, only one, bearing the name of the Empress Irene, can be dated—to between 1081 and 1118—and this may have belonged to the first *Pala*, ordered from Constantinople by the Doge. Other enamels were probably made in Venice or brought there from Constantinople after its sack in 1204, the squalid climax of the Fourth Crusade.

3
Plaques intended for a reliquary or book-cover.
a
St Paul, Byzantine, 11-12th century.
Gold and cloisonné enamel, his name inscribed in Greek. Probably originally part of a series of saints and apostles, and closely related to the plaque of St Peter in the D'Arcy Gallery of Art, Chicago.
w. and h. 3.2 cm.
4910-1901
b
Christ, Byzantine or South Russian, 11-12th century.
Gold and cloisonné enamel.
dia. 1.9 cm.
M.71-1934

4
Plaque of a dancing girl.
Gold with cloisonné enamel.
Thought to be associated with the crown of Emperor Constantine Monomachos (1042-55).
Comparable panels from his crown are in the National Museum, Budapest.
h. 10.5 cm. w. 5 cm.
M.325-1921

5
The Beresford-Hope reliquary cross, Italian, 9th century.
Gold and cloisonné enamel mounted in silver-gilt.
The Virgin in the centre is shown between busts of St Peter and St Andrew; above and below are St John the Baptist and St Paul. On the other side Christ is represented on the Cross between the Virgin and St John the Evangelist. The relic, which has disappeared, might have been of one of the saints depicted, or a fragment of the Cross. Intended to be worn as a pectoral cross.
h. 8.5 cm. w. 5.5 cm.
265-1886

6
Votice offering in the form of an annular cross, Lombardic, 9th century.
Bronze, with the remains of its original silver sheathing, overlaid with plaques of cloisonné enamel on copper-gilt, and cabuchon pastes.
Although nothing of comparable type survives, this piece was perhaps intended to be suspended over an altar.
w. 14.1 cm. l. 29.8 cm.
100-1882

7
Plaques with the symbols of St Matthew and St John, Rhenish (Trier), late 10th century.
Copper-gilt, formed of superimposed plates, the front one with the design cut out and filled in with cloisonné enamel.
Probably from a book-cover, or reliquary. It is rare to find cloisonné enamel on base metal at this date.
h. 5.7 cm. w. 5.3 cm.
M.517 & a-1924

8

Sion book-cover, German (Trier?). The central figure of Christ and the gilt borders date from the 12th century. The plaques of cloisonné are late 10th century, partly restored in the 19th century. Beechwood, overlaid with embossed gold sheets, stones and cloisonné enamel plaques on gold, covering a 10th-century Evangelistary (Gospel readings for the Mass).

The cover was stolen from the treasury of St Maurice d'Agaune in the 14th century, and later acquired by the monastery of Sion in Switzerland, who sold it in 1851. It later passed through the collections of the Marquis de Ganay and Spitzer.

l. 25.4 cm. w. 22 cm.

567-1893

Western European Enamels

The influence of Byzantine cloisonné enamels on the style and technique of Western goldsmiths was pervasive. Italy, an obvious geographical intermediary between Western Europe and Constantinople, may well have been an important disseminator of Byzantine enamelled products. It is possible that cloisonné enamel was being produced in Italy as early as the sixth century, as a result of contact with Byzantine jewellers working in the Italian territories of the Emperor Justinian (527-65). The importance of Byzantine iconographical and stylistic models is reflected in the pectoral cross, now in the Museo Sacro in the Vatican, which is associated with Pope Paschal I (817-824), and may have been made in Rome. The superficial resemblance to it, in form and style, of the Beresford-Hope cross [plate 5] may argue for a similar date and provenance. Against this must be considered its technical similarity—especially in the range of enamel colours used—to the Byzantine Fieschi-Morgan reliquary in the Metropolitan Museum, New York. Another important contemporary work, probably by Italian goldsmiths, is the gold and cloisonné enamel 'iron' crown in the Cathedral of Monza, whose crude leaf forms resemble those on the unique bronze and cloisonné votive offering in the V&A, which was probably intended to hang over an altar [plate 6]. Elsewhere in Europe, the influence of the Byzantine cloisonné style is less apparent, owing perhaps to the residual survival of a native champlevé technique. Yet the famous late ninth-century jewel associated with King Alfred the Great in the Ashmolean Museum, Oxford, has a gold mount of markedly Anglo-Saxon style decorated with a figure in a cloisonné enamel of a sturdiness remote from Byzantine refinement. The eighth-century Ardagh chalice in the National Museum Dublin reveals what seems to be a specifically Irish technique. Its enamel bosses have the superficial appearance of cloisonné work but in fact consist of a metal fretwork filled with enamel, a technique more allied to the native Celtic champlevé tradition. The eighth-century Lindau gospel-cover in the Pierpont Morgan Library, New York, and the Enger reliquary in the Staatliche Museum, Berlin, are probably German; both are decorated with cloisonné biting beasts in a style unknown to Byzantine art. Most

9

Reliquary cross, Anglo-Saxon, late 10th century.
Gold, on a wooden base, the figure of Christ in walrus ivory, the titulus and medallions depicting the symbols of the Evangelists in cloisonné enamel.
A fragmentary inscription around the edge lists the relics formerly contained in the cavity beneath the figure, which included a fragment of the True Cross.
A dried human finger, possibly female, is all that now remains.
The enamels are unique in Anglo-Saxon art of this period, and may have been made by a goldsmith familiar with German work.
From the Soltikoff collection.
h. 18.5 cm. w. 13.4 cm.
7943-1862

unusually, the Lindau goldsmith has used champlevé enamel as well as cloisonné.

In 972 Otto II, the German Emperor, married Princess Theophanu, niece of the Byzantine Emperor John I Tzimisces and with her, legend claims, came goldsmiths and enamellers from Constantinople. The efflorescence of fine German cloisonné work at this time was more probably a result of the increasing patronage of the Court and the Church. Owing to this stimulus, and in particular to commissions from Archbishop Egbert (977-93), the city of Trier, capital of an archdiocese, became an important producer of gold cloisonné work. Its products, often characterised by stylised leaf-work, include the sumptuous book covers from Echternach, now in in the Germanisches Nationalmuseum, Nuremberg, and Trier Cathedral's reliquary of St Andrew's sandal. Two copper cloisonné plaques in the V&A [plate 7] bear a strong resemblance to Trier work and the enamels on the Sion book-cover [plate 8] may also be from there.

Other manufacturing centres whose output was stimulated by ecclesiastical demand were Mainz, Regensburg, Cologne and Essen. The Cathedral treasury at Essen still holds many of its city's products, amongst the most splendid of which are two altar crosses made for the Abbess Matilda (d.1011). The delicacy of their cell-work and their range of colours are not unlike those of the small Evangelist medallions in gold cloisonné, often called Anglo-Saxon, on the cross in plate 9. One of the greatest surviving pieces of medieval regalia, the crown now in the Kunsthistorisches Museum, Vienna, may also have been made at Essen for the coronation of the Holy Roman Emperor Otto the Great in 962; its technique and form reflect a Byzantine inspiration.

An important later example of cloisonné is the early eleventh century gold St Severinus medallion in the Diocesan Museum, Cologne, all that remains of the great shrine dedicated to that Saint. The use of translucent as well as opaque enamel, particularly the difficult colour red, demonstrates an exceptional mastery of the medium.

The only known treatise on metalworking from this period, *De Diversis Artibus*, was written early in the twelfth century by Theophilus Presbiter, thought to be the German goldsmith Roger of Helmarshausen. It describes the technique of making enamel (*electrsm*), clearly of the cloisonné type, and ways of obtaining various colours by grinding up the tesserae of Roman mosaics. But Theophilus was evidently a late practitioner of a technique in decline, for by the late eleventh or early twelfth century champlevé enamel on copper had become fashionable. The change may have been due to various factors: the sheer expense of cloisonné, a process best suited for use on gold or silver; a shortage of precious metals; and an enormously increased demand for church vessels, stimulated by the large number of new religious foundations.

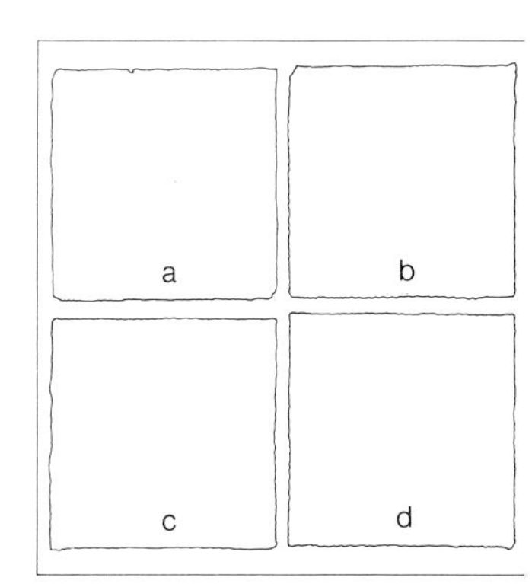

10

Group of plaques, perhaps from an altarpiece or shrine, Mosan, 3rd quarter of the 12th century. Copper gilt with champlevé enamel and some details in cloisonné.
They show: a) a man on a camel b) Samson and the lion c) the Ascension of Alexander d) Moses and the brazen serpent (Numbers 21.9). Other plaques from the group are now in the British Museum (Namaan bathing in the Jordan); New York, Metropolitan Museum (the Baptism, the Crucifixion, the Holy Women at the Tomb, Pentecost); Paris, Louvre (a Centaur-Man killing a dragon, and Ss Sebastian, Tranquillinus, and Livinus).

The group perhaps formed part of a large scheme showing the complete Life of Christ, with typological subjects. It has been suggested that they come from Suger's altar cross, but this seems unlikely since the cross was probably decorated only with Christ's Passion and Resurrection.
The plaque of Moses and the brazen serpent has lost all its enamel, and clearly demonstrates the depth of engraving necessary to hold the enamel, as well as the surface roughening or 'keying' which was intended to provide better adhesion.
10.2 cm. sq.
a–c) Lent by Lt Col J. Harding-Rolls
d) M.59-1952

Twelfth Century Enamels in Western Europe

The period from about 1050 to soon after 1200 was one of increasing prosperity, the result of relative peace after centuries of barbarian invasions. Throughout Western Europe there was a revival of large-scale building and a rebirth of architectural sculpture. These activities provide a key to the dominant artistic style of the period, in which ornament is subordinated to structure. Byzantine art still exercised a strong influence on the enamels of the period, as evidenced by the formal frontal presentation of the figures and the stylised modelling of their garments.

The twelfth century Church's need for liturgical objects—crosses, candlesticks, pyxes, reliquaries and croziers—stimulated the production of champlevé enamels in such traditional metalworking centres as the Meuse and Rhine valleys, as well as in France and Spain. The question of which centre first made enamels of this new type has long been disputed: a matter further complicated by the effects of patronage, which might draw together to one place craftsmen from various regions to work on a particular commission.

1 1
Composite altar cross. The central plaques back and front (Christ in Majesty and the Lamb of God, the figure of Christ) and the cross-foot, North German (Lower Saxony), second half of the 12th century. The remaining plaques Mosan, second half of the twelfth century. The copper gilt leaves and flowers on the arms of the cross are of the 15th century, when the whole was probably assembled.
Champlevé, with details in cloisonné enamel on copper-gilt, mounted on a wooden base.
At the extremities are four Old Testament types of the Redemption: Aaron marking a house with the blood of the Passover (Exodus 12.7) Jacob blessing the sons of Joseph (Genesis 48) Elijah and the widow Sarepta (I Kings 17.8-16) Moses and the brazen serpent (Numbers 21.9 and John 3.14).
The iconography of the Mosan plaques is close to that of a cross in the British Museum, which shows in addition the Return of the Spies from the Promised Land (Numbers 13.25). This scene may originally have taken the place of the present Lamb of God plaque on this cross. Said to have come from a church in Cologne.
h. 66.1 cm. w. 41.9 cm.
7234-1860

12
Reliquary triptych of the True Cross, Mosan, last quarter of the 12th century.
Plaques of embossed copper gilt and of champlevé enamel on copper, on a foundation of oak.
At the top, Christ in Majesty; in the centre, a glazed receptacle containing the relics, with angels at the sides holding instruments of the Passion, the angels of Mercy and Justice above, and a plaque with the Crucifixion; below, symbols of the Four Evangelists. At the bottom, the visit of the holy women to the Sepulchre and a large 9th-century crystal engraved with the Crucifixion, set in filigree. On the wings, the Twelve Apostles. The motive of angels carrying the reliquary panel of the Cross is found also on triptychs at Liège, and the Petit Palais, Paris.
From the Soltikoff Collection.
h. 57.8 cm. w. 63.6 cm.
7947-1862

13

The Alton Towers triptych, Rhenish (Cologne), second half of the 12th century, with 19th century additions.

Copper gilt with champlevé enamel, bordered by strips of copper gilt, partly decorated with brown varnish, set on a wooden base.

The theme of the Redemption is illustrated by scenes from the New Testament on the central panel, which are paralleled on the wings by scenes from the Old Testament considered to prefigure them.

The Crucifixion is thus placed between the Sacrifice of Isaac by Abraham (Genesis 22.9) and Moses and the brazen serpent (Numbers 21.9); the Holy Women at the Sepulchre between Jonah and the whale (Jonah 1.17) and Elisha raising a dead man (2 Kings 12.21); the Harrowing of Hell between the catching of Leviathan (Job 41.1) and Samson carrying the gates of Gaza (Judges 16.3).

The triptych has certain stylistic similarities to the portable altar of St Mauritius in Siegburg.

From the collection of the Earls of Shrewsbury.

h. 36.2 cm. w. 47.6 cm.

4757-1858

There is, however, no doubt that Suger (*c.*1081–1151), great prelate and patron of the arts, summoned to his abbey of St Denis outside Paris goldsmiths from Lorraine (*aurifabri Lotharingi*) to make the six-foot high altar cross consecrated by the Pope in 1147. Its pedestal was enamelled with episodes from the life of Christ juxtaposed with 'typological' scenes—that is, Old Testament incidents whose theme was thought to prefigure those in the New Testament. The cross has perished, although the cross base in the St Omer Museum is thought to be a later diminutive version. Suger's account confirms, at that early date, the skill and reputation of goldsmiths from Lorraine, which then included the ecclesiastical and metalworking centres of Liège and Maastricht in the Meuse valley—hence the generic term 'Mosan enamels'. Moreover, the iconography of the abbot's cross pedestal testifies to the early interest of Mosan enamellers in complex theological themes inspired by the liturgy; this continued to be a characteristic of their work, in marked contrast with contemporary products from France and Spain.

14
Plaque of the prophet Jonah from the Darmstadt reliquary, Rhenish, second half of the 12th century.
Copper gilt with champlevé enamel.
Jonah holding a tablet with an inscription from Jonah 1.12.
It is the missing plaque from a 12-sided reliquary now in Darmstadt, and is engraved on the reverse with the letter E, probably a workshop assembly mark.
h. 12.4 cm. w. 6.3 cm.
4097-1857

15
The Eltenberg reliquary, Rhenish (Cologne), last quarter of the 12th century.
Copper and bronze gilt, with champlevé enamel and ivory carvings, on a wooden foundation.
Around the dome are seated Christ and 11 apostles with, below, 16 figures of prophets who hold inscribed scrolls. Four ivory plaques depict the Nativity, the Three Magi, the Crucifixion and the Holy Women at the Sepulchre; the first two of these are 19th-century replacements copied from the similar reliquary in Berlin. The latter once enclosed the head of St Gregory Nazianzus, and it is probable that the Eltenberg reliquary likewise contained a substantial relic. At the time of the French Revolution, the reliquary was in the Benedictine nunnery at Eltenberg on the German/Dutch border. At the suppression of the nunnery in the early 19th century, the last canoness hid the reliquary in the chimney of her house. Thereafter it passed to several owners, including the dealer Jacob Cohen of Anholt, and Prince Florentin of Salm-Salm whose restorer, F. Schultz, of Anholt, repaired it; it was probably again repaired on behalf of the dealer Schmitz of Cologne.
h. 54.5 cm. l. 51 cm. w. 51 cm.
7650-1861

16
Spandrel plaques from a shrine, Rhenish (?Cologne) under Mosan influence, 3rd quarter of the 12th century.
Copper gilt with champlevé enamel, and cloisonné details.
Probably placed originally between the arcades on the sides of a shrine. Half figures of angels hold texts from the Beatitudes, a) Blessed are the meek (St Matthew 5.5) b) Blessed are the pure in heart (St Matthew 5.8).
This subject occurs, amongst other places, on the Alexander head reliquary, and on the Mosan influenced candelabrum at Aachen cathedral. Plaques of this shape, showing personifications of Religion and Faith, are in the British Museum.
Stylistically the plaques may indicate the influence of the workshop which produced the Shrine of St Maurinus in the church of St Pantaleon, Cologne.
h. 7.6 cm. w. 8.9 cm.
6816,7-1860

Most surviving Mosan enamels seem to date from the brief period 1140-80. Generally speaking the figures are enamelled on a copper-gilt ground, but heads and hands are usually reserved in the metal, with only the engraved outlines being filled with a blue or red enamel. A wide range of colours is used with a predilection for greens, yellows and a distinctive turquoise.

The earliest dateable extant Mosan piece is the head reliquary of Pope Alexander (now in the Musées Royaux, Brussels) made in 1145 for Abbot Wibald of Stavelot. Wibald also commissioned in about 1150 the vast Remaclus retable or altarpiece—of which only two medallions, now in the Museum für Kunsthandwerk, Frankfurt and the Staatliche Museum, Berlin, remain—and probably the Stavelot triptych of 1155-8, in the Morgan Library, New York. All are likely to have been made in one workshop. A series of square Mosan plaques [plate 10], now dispersed between the Metropolitan Museum, the Louvre, the British Museum and the V&A, may have originated from one object, possibly an altar retable. Godefroid de Claire, or of Huy, a goldsmith renowned amongst his contemporaries, has been credited with some or all of this work; unfortunately, the only piece certainly by him, the shrine of Ss Domitian and Mangold in Huy, is stylistically dissimilar. Rare features of this group are the use of the translucent colours green and ox-blood in addition to the normal opaque enamels, and the occasional employment of cloisonné for fine detail. Work of a slightly later period includes an altar cross in the V&A [plate 11]—similar in iconography, although not in style, to one in the British Museum—and the *armillae* (arm-ornaments) depicting the Crucifixion and the Resurrection, probably part of the Imperial vestments of the Holy Roman Emperor, Frederick Barbarossa (1155-90), and now divided between the Louvre and the Germanisches Museum, Nuremberg.

17
Portable altar, North German, late 12th century.
Copper gilt with champlevé enamel, on an oak foundation.
On the top, the Crucifixion, with figures representing the Church and Synagogue; around the sides, half figures of the 12 Apostles.
h. 8.3 cm. l. 17.1 cm. w. 10.1 cm.
4524-1858

18
The Masters plaque, English, mid-12th century.
Copper gilt with champlevé enamel.
Christ surrounded by angels above, and the damned in hell below. Inscribed on the back, 'Given to Thomas Kerrich by Robert Masters, D.D., Aug. 23rd 1796'. It was acquired from the heirs of Albert Hartshorne, antiquary, grandson of Kerrich.
h. 13.8 cm. w. 8.9 cm.
M.209-1925

19
Plaques from a shrine of St Peter and St Paul, English, last quarter of the 12th century.
Copper gilt with champlevé enamel.

a
St Paul disputing with the Greeks and Jews (Acts of the Apostles 17. 16-32, 19. 1-20).
From the Webb collection.
h. 8.6 cm. w. 12.7 cm.
223-1874

b
St Paul escaping in a basket down the walls of Damascus (II Corinthians 11.32, Acts 9.19-25).
From the John Edward Taylor collection.

The other five surviving plaques are in Dijon (St Peter receiving the keys and St Peter and St Paul before Nero), Lyons (Conversion of St Paul), Nuremberg (St Peter walking on the water) and New York (St Paul seated amongst disciples).
h. 8.5 cm. w. 12.7 cm.
M. 312-1926

20a

Watercolour of the Warwick Ciborium.
Attributed to John Talman (d.1726).
The ciborium as it was before being damaged in the fire of 1871 at Warwick Castle, and soon after its discovery in a brazier's shop in 1717.
London, Society of Antiquaries (*Harley Collection* vol.2, p.30).
The remains of the Warwick ciborium (English, 1150-75) are in the V & A collection (M.159-1919). Only fragments of enamel have survived; its present appearance, however, demonstrates the surface preparation, normally invisible, that was necessary before the enamel was applied. The cover has long been missing, but the scenes on the bowl suggest what the cover might have depicted:

Bowl:	*Cover:*
1. Moses and the burning bush	1. The Annunciation?
2. Sacrifice of Cain and Abel	2. The Presentation?
3. The circumcision of Isaac	3. The Baptism of Christ?
4. Isaac carrying logs	4. Christ carrying the cross?
5. The sacrifice of Isaac by Abraham	5. The Crucifixion?
6. Jonah and the whale	6. Holy women at the Sepulchre?

20b

The Balfour Ciborium, English, 1150-75.
Champlevé enamel and copper gilt.
It depicts complementary scenes from the Old Testament (bowl) and the New (cover) on the theme of the Redemption, a subject appropriate for a eucharistic container. The scenes are as follows:

Bowl:	*Cover:*
1. The circumcision of Isaac	1. The Baptism of Christ
2. Isaac carrying logs	2. Christ carrying the cross
3. The sacrifice of Isaac by Abraham	3. Crucifixion
4. Samson and the harlot of Gaza	4. Holy women at the Sepulchre
5. David slaying the bear	5. The harrowing of Hell
6. Elijah's ascension	6. Christ's Ascension

The similarities between the Warwick, Balfour and Pierpont Morgan ciboria are striking. Two scenes, Isaac's circumcision and Isaac and the logs, are iconographically very rare but appeared in the 12th-century wall-paintings in Worcester cathedral chapter house and in the choir of Peterborough cathedral. Further evidence for an English origin for the ciboria lies in the similarity of their unusually elaborate floral scrolls to those on certain English sculptures.
h. 18.3 cm. d. 16.5 cm.
M.1-1981

20c

The Pierpont Morgan or Malmesbury ciborium, English, 1150-75.
Champlevé enamel and copper gilt.
This is the third and central member of the group of ciboria. It shares scenes with both the others, and shows the following episodes on its bowl and cover:

Bowl:	*Cover:*
1. Aaron's flowering rod	1a. The Nativity
2. Sacrifice of Cain and Abel	2b. The Presentation of Christ in the Temple
3. The circumcision of Isaac	3b. Baptism of Christ
4. Isaac carrying the logs	4b. Christ carrying the cross
5. Moses and the brazen serpent	5c. Crucifixion
6. Samson and the harlot of Gaza	6c. Holy women at the Sepulchre

h. 19 cm. d. 16.2 cm.
New York, Pierpont Morgan Library.

The Lower Rhineland, and especially Cologne, was another major producer of champlevé enamels in the twelfth century. Rhenish work is characterised by figures engraved on the metal and gilt, with only the background enamelled; the range of colours is narrower than that of Mosan work, with a preference for greens and blues. The workshop of Eilbertus of Cologne (active about 1140-70) may have been responsible for reviving permanently the technique of champlevé in Northern Europe; it produced the portable altar from the Guelph treasure, now in the Staatliche Museum, Berlin, on which the champlevé figures of prophets seem in close imitation of the cloisonné technique, since prominent metal ridges separate each colour.

The Alton Towers triptych in the V&A [plate 12] was possibly made in Cologne; it is decorated with an elaborate typological scheme—similar to that described by Suger—which compares closely with contemporary manuscript illumination.

21
Liberal Arts casket, English (?), late 12th century. Copper gilt with champlevé enamel; some of the greens and blues are transparent.
The Liberal Arts—grammar, rhetoric, logic, music, arithmetic, geometry and astronomy—constituted the basic syllabus in a medieval school. The casket is decorated with personifications of them as well as with figures of Philosophy, Nature and Knowledge. Stylistically, it resembles three plaques decorated with baptismal scenes formerly in the Von Hirsch collection. From the Soltikoff collection.
h. 6.3 cm. w. 5.5 cm.
7955-1862.

Some of the most important Rhenish enamels show Mosan influence; for example, the vast house-shaped shrine, made about 1170, to contain the relics of St Heribert at Deutz. The form of this reliquary became a prototype for many later examples. Another Cologne workshop, formerly identified as that of a craftsman named Fredericus, produced pieces characterised by fleshy scalloped leaves; amongst them is the tower-shaped Darmstadt reliquary, from which there is a plaque in the V &A [plate 14], the St Gregorius portable altar in Siegburg abbey and a plaque, perhaps from an altar, in the Condé Museum, Chantilly. A related workshop may have produced the nearly twin reliquaries of which one, the Eltenberg [plate 15], is now in the V &A and the other, part of the Guelph treasure, is in Berlin; both take the form of a miniature domed church on a Greek cross plan, enamelled and set with ivories.

By contrast with the work of his contemporaries, that of Nicholas of Verdun (active about 1181-1205) shows a precocious and dynamic naturalism, inspired perhaps both by classical and Byzantine models, and is clearly a precursor of the Gothic style. He probably trained in the Mosan region and later worked in Aachen and Cologne, for in style and iconography his work seems to be a fusion of the Mosan and the Rhenish. His first documented work, the pulpit made for Klosterneuburg Abbey in Austria, is one of the supreme masterpieces of the twelfth century. It originally consisted of 45 plaques, each decorated with an individual scene in which the figures are engraved and gilt on a champlevé enamel ground. Following damage by fire in 1330, the pulpit was remodelled into a retable with the addition of six figure-scenes in the central panel. The plaques are arranged in three rows and together make up the most ambitious twelfth-century typological programme to have survived.

English metalwork of the twelfth century closely followed developments on the Continent and the style of enamelling in particular was influenced by Mosan work. Early links between the two regions may have been formed by the presence in England, both before and after the Conquest, of Lorrainers holding high ecclesiastical office. The V &A is fortunate to possess several of the very few surviving enamels; the earliest is the Masters' plaque [plate 18], whose style compares with that of English manuscripts of about 1150. In the British Museum are two enamelled plaques, one of which depicts Henry of Blois, Bishop of Winchester (1129-71), and may come from the shrine of St Swithun, made in about 1150 to contain the saint's relics. Of a series of plaques, probably from a shrine, which illustrate the lives of St Peter and Paul [plate 19], seven survive. The similarity of their iconography to that of the mosaics in the Cappella Palatina in Palermo, and in Monreale, may well be accounted for by the influence of a common prototype, such as a Byzantine manuscript. There were strong links between England and Sicily at that period.

22
Ecclesiastical items.
Limoges, 13th century.
A typical group of Limoges products, characterised by the use of a deep, strong blue, and stylised floral motifs.

a
Pastoral staff.
Virgin and Child (front) and Christ in Majesty.
h. 29.2 cm. dia. 10.7 cm.
M.17-1913

b
Candlestick.
h. 18.4 cm. w. 11.4 cm.
4912-1901

c
Chrismatory (receptable for holy oils).
h. 10.2 cm. w. 7.6 cm.
186-1866

d
Reliquary.
Intended for the relics of a saint, perhaps one of those depicted on it.
From the Salting Collection.
h. 26 cm. l. 26.9 cm. w. 12.1 cm.
M.572-1910

23
Eucharistic dove, Limoges, 13th century.
Copper-gilt with champlevé enamel.
Symbol of the Holy Spirit, the dove was used for keeping the consecrated sacrament in reserve. It was suspended above the altar by means of chains attached to the base and could be lowered when needed.
These eucharistic doves were a particular specialty of the Limoges workshops and many examples survive.
h. 18.2 cm.
Washington National Gallery of Art (Widener Collection no. C-8)

A group of three enamelled ciboria (vessels to contain the reserved sacrament) combine Mosan stylistic features with the luxuriant blossoms and vinescrolls typical of contemporary English manuscripts and sculpture. Their unusual iconography is found in some English wall-paintings, and in sculptures at Malmesbury Abbey. Two of the ciboria, that recently bought by the V&A from Lord Balfour of Burleigh [plate 20], and the one in the Pierpont Morgan Library, New York, must come from the same workshop, so similar are they in design and colour range. The third, the Warwick ciborium in the V&A, has lost most of its enamel and its cover; as in the other two vessels, this last would undoubtedly have been enamelled with scenes from the New Testament, in juxtaposition with their Old Testament precursors on the bowl, all illustrating Christ's sacrifice and redemption—a theme entirely appropriate for

24
Valence casket, Limoges or English, about 1300.
Copper-gilt and champlevé enamel.
Decorated with the armorial bearings of the Valence family (Earls of Pembroke), the Royal house of England, the Dukes of Brittany (Dreux), the families of Angoulême, Brabant and Lacy (Earls of Lincoln). The casket was perhaps made to safeguard jewels, and may have belonged either to Aymer de Valence (d.1324) or to his father William (d.1296), whose partly enamelled tomb in Westminster Abbey is comparable. Another enamelled tomb, made for Walter de Merton, Bishop of Rochester (d.1276), was commissioned from a Limoges craftsman named John, so the casket, which is unique, may have been made either in Limoges or in England. A contemporary enamelled cup lid survives in All Souls College, Oxford, and is decorated with arms associated with Aymer de Valence's wife, Beatrice de Nesle.
h. 8.8 cm. w. 17.6 cm. l. 13.3 cm.
4-1865

a vessel intended for the eucharist. Certain scenes on all three ciboria are so alike as to argue a common workshop, evidence of whose iconographical patternbook is found in descriptions of lost wall paintings once at Peterborough and Worcester.

In France, the beginnings of the champlevé enamel industry, which had become active in Limoges by the late twelfth century, remain obscure. Some early enamels attributed to Limoges are very similar in design and colour scheme to pieces probably of Spanish origin; but controversy over whether the style originated in Southern France or Northern Spain remains unresolved. In the early twelfth century, the relationship between the architecture and sculpture, as well as the metalwork of the two regions, was very close; this may perhaps be explained by the existence of travelling workshops patronised by both areas. Certainly, some later features of 'Limoges' enamels, such as backgrounds of *vermicule* (engraved arabesque) and Cufic decorative borders, are so clearly Arabic in origin that Spanish influence cannot be doubted.

The reliquary casket in the French abbey of Conques is covered in champlevé medallions, enamelled in obvious imitation of gold cloisonné, and its probable date, between 1107 and 1118, makes it amongst the earliest extant works in the new style of enamelling. The Spanish/French controversy is epitomised by the very similar decoration on the Champagnat casket in the Metropolitan Museum, and on the San Domingo de Silos casket and altar frontal in Burgos Museum; the Champagnat casket shows St Martial, patron saint of Limoges, whereas St Dominic, patron of Silos, appears on the Burgos casket. All three caskets date from between 1125 and 1150, and show figures and animals enamelled on a reserved gilt ground. Of similar type is the large plaque at Le Mans, made for the tomb of Geoffrey Plantagenet soon after his death in 1151. It shows considerable technical skill: the figure and face are enamelled on a gilt ground itself also partly enamelled.

In complete stylistic contrast is a casket-shaped shrine of St Calmin, made for the abbot of Mozac in 1168-81. Here, nearly all the figures are in gilt-bronze relief against a brilliant dark-blue ground sprinkled with multicoloured roundels, leaves and stripes—a style that was to become typical of a good deal of later Limoges work. Many of the pieces in the V&A are of this type. In terms of the quantity and variety of their output, the Limoges enamellers were unsurpassed, but, inevitably, the quality was often mediocre. Wares for ecclesiastical and domestic use were widely exported from Limoges; particular specialities included reliquary caskets of St Thomas à Becket, showing his murder, and eucharistic doves, made to hold the reserved sacrament suspended over the altar [plate 23]. Items for personal use included portable folding candlesticks, caskets [plate 24], badges (many decorated with the owner's arms) and *gemellions*, which were used in pairs for washing hands at meals.

The Gothic Period

Although the enamellers of Limoges continued to produce objects of champlevé on copper throughout the thirteenth and well into the fourteenth century, metalworkers elsewhere showed themselves less bound by tradition. In the thirteenth century champlevé enamel was generally eclipsed in popularity by other forms of surface decoration, particularly filigree and niello. The greater naturalism characteristic of the Gothic style was perhaps more difficult to achieve in the somewhat rigid and stylised medium of champlevé enamel.

The increasing use of precious metals in enamelled objects from the late thirteenth century onwards seems partly to be due to the growing wealth of the aristocracy and the middle classes, and partly to the greater availability of the metals themselves. The new technique of basse-taille enamel could only be used on gold or silver. It may have been invented either in France or in Italy, but the earliest example to survive is on a chalice in Assisi, made and signed by Guccio di Mannaia, for Pope Nicholas IV (1288-92).

Numerous chalices, crosses and reliquaries embellished with plaques of basse-taille enamel survive from Northern Italy [plate 25], although the enamel is frequently damaged. Amongst the finest is the large reliquary in Orvieto Cathedral made by Ugolino di Vieri in 1338, decorated with dozens of plaques of brilliant translucent enamel illustrating the life of Christ; the modelling of the figures heralds the Renaissance.

Goldsmiths throughout Europe were quick to follow the fashion for basse-taille, and produced quantities of lavish work for both personal and ecclesiastical use. Because of its high intrinsic value, much translucent enamelwork was subsequently consigned to the melting pot, leaving us only tantalising inventory descriptions. In Northern Europe the artistic lead, held by Germany and the Low Countries in the twelfth century, passed in the Gothic era to France, where the first European guild of goldsmiths and silversmiths was founded in Paris in 1202. An outstanding group of Parisian translucent enamels includes the reliquary commissioned by Queen Jeanne d'Evreux in 1339 and now in the Louvre, the ewer, chalice and paten dated 1333 in Copenhagen, and the altarpiece triptych in

25
Italian church plate.

a
Processional cross, Italian (Tuscan), mid-14th century. Silver, parcel gilt, set with plaques originally covered with translucent enamel on silver.
Flanking the Crucifixion are the Virgin and St Mark, with Christ in Majesty above and Mary Magdalen below. On the back the Resurrection is flanked by St Luke and St Matthew with St John above and St Peter below.
From the Rutschi and Hildburgh collections.
h. 48.2 cm. w. 36.2 cm.
M.9-1951

b
Chalice, Italian (Sienese), first half of the 14th century. Gilt copper, the bowl of silver, set with plaques of translucent enamel on silver.
On the foot: the Crucifixion, the Virgin and St John, St Nicholas (?), St Lawrence and St Martin. On the knop are: Christ, St Peter, St Paul, St Francis of Assisi, St Stephen and a bishop saint. The inscription reads '*+FRATE IACHOMO MONDUSI+DE SENA+ME FECIT*'. Sienese goldsmiths produced a large number of chalices of this type and examples survive in the British Museum, the Fitzwilliam Museum, Cambridge, various museums in the USA and France, as well as in the Italian churches for which they were originally made.
From the Webb collection.
h. 21.6 cm. dia. 15.2 cm.
237-1874

26
Morse (brooch for an ecclesiastical vestment) North Italian, 1325-50. Translucent enamel on silver, set into a frame of gilt copper.
Showing the Annunciation, the delicacy of the engraving bears some resemblance to the work of Ugolino di Vieri, whose masterpiece is still in Orvieto Cathedral. A companion piece showing San Galgano is in the Cluny Museum, Paris.
From the Webb collection.
dia. 7.9 cm.
221-1874

Milan. Of the great quantity of translucent enamel made for domestic use, including cups, jugs, wine fountains and jewellery, little has survived. The masterpiece, however, of French translucent enamelling is the 'Royal Gold Cup', now in the British Museum, which is supreme in both technical mastery and aesthetic appeal. Made of gold, enamelled with scenes from the life of St Agnes, it was almost certainly made between 1380 and 1390 for a member of the French royal house, whose devotion to St Agnes is well documented.

English work of the Gothic period was almost entirely destroyed at the Dissolution of the Monasteries in the sixteenth century. The Swinburne pyx [plate 30] is a rare exception; despite the loss of its enamel, it is of historical importance because the engraving upon it closely resembles the illustrations in an English manuscript of

27
St Laurence, French or Spanish, late 13th century.
Copper gilt with champlevé enamel.
St Laurence holds a grid-iron, his symbol. The plaque may be from a reliquary, another part of which—a plaque of St James—is in the Walters Art Gallery, Baltimore. The castles in the border may be heraldic allusions to the arms of Castile in Spain. Blanche of Castile married King Louis VIII of France in 1200. From the Spitzer and Salting collections.
h. 11.6 cm. w. 6 cm.
M. 571-1910

*c.*1310–25, written for a female ancestor of the Swinburne family, who appear to have owned the pyx since the fourteenth century. Some of the extant miniature altarpieces intended for private use [plate 31] may also be of English origin and are similar to contemporary manuscripts. Of those in the V&A collection, the triptych on loan from Campion Hall, Oxford [plate 31c], is of particular interest; it displays St Edmund, patron of English kings, so prominently that its English origin cannot be doubted. The enamelled crozier given to New College, Oxford, by William of Wykeham (d.1404) may well also be English. Of domestic pieces, the most handsome are the King's Lynn cup of about 1340, enamelled with fashionably-dressed figures of the time, and owned by the Corporation of King's Lynn; the Savernake horn [plate 33] in the British Museum, its silver bands enamelled with birds, beasts

28
Pyxes, French, early 14th century.
Copper-gilt, with champlevé enamel.
Pyxes are containers for the reserved sacrament.

a
On the outside, the 12 Apostles; on the inside, a man's head and grotesque monsters.
From the Soltikoff and Morland collections.
h. 10.1 cm. dia. 10.1 cm.
82-1866

b
On the outside, the 12 Apostles; on the inside, base, Christ in Majesty and the symbols of the Evangelists, lid, St Eustace and two children.
From the Debruge-Dumenil, Soltikoff and Morland collections.
h. 10.1 cm. dia. 8.9 cm.
183-1866

and figures, and its 'baldric' or carrying strap enamelled with the arms of the Earls of Moray; and the Bute mazer (on loan to the Museum of Antiquities, Edinburgh), embellished with the enamelled arms of Scottish noble families of the fourteenth century.

In Germany, there were important workshops on the Upper Rhine, probably centred upon Basle and Constance. Basle may have produced the great house-shrine of St Mark (1303-5), still preserved nearby at Reichenau, which is decorated with a mixture of champlevé and translucent enamel, the Sigmaringen chalice of 1320-40 in Baltimore, and the Reichenau crozier, dated 1351, in the V & A [plate 35]. Elsewhere in Germany Cologne continued to be a major metalworking centre and produced the earliest-known example of German translucent enamelling—the monstrance-reliquary of about 1300 made for Graf von Isenburg—as well as many pieces still in the Aachen cathedral treasury.

In the late fourteenth and early fifteenth century, under the lavish patronage of the kings of France and the Dukes of Burgundy, goldsmiths developed further refinements to the technique of enamelling. The effect of stained glass in miniature was created by the difficult plique-à-jour technique, the only surviving medieval

29
Reliquary-pendant, French (Parisian?), late 14th century.
Translucent enamel on silver-gilt.
Showing St Catherine of Alexandria. The relic consists of a small piece of cloth held in place by a piece of crystal at the back. The style of the figure bears some resemblance to those on the Royal Gold Cup in the British Museum.
From the J. E. Taylor collection.
h. 6.7 cm. w. 5.3 cm.
M.350-1912

30
Swinburne Pyx, English, 1310-25. Silver gilt, formerly covered in translucent enamel.
The container is decorated with the Lamb of God underneath, the head of Christ inside and a series of canopies on the outside. The lid shows on the inside the Nativity and on the outside the Virgin and Child; both scenes appear to have been copied from the same book of designs as was used by the illuminators of two manuscripts, Cambridge University Library ms Dd.4.17, and Cambridge Corpus Christi College ms 53, written for East Anglican clients early in the 14th century.
dia. 5.6 cm. h. 2.9 cm.
M. 15-1950

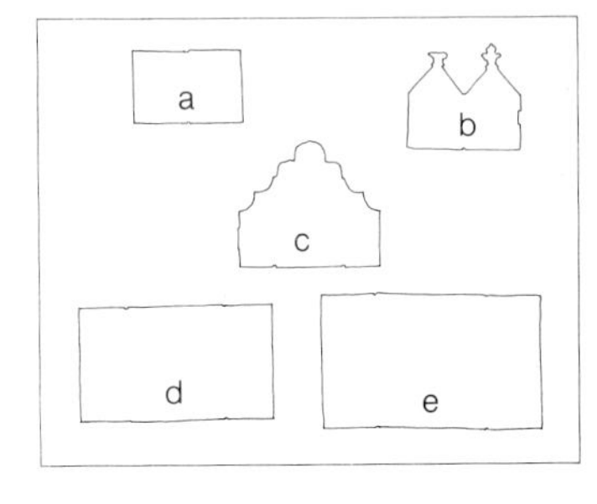

31
Group of altarpieces.

These tiny enamels were probably made for wealthy and devout patrons, for use in their private chapels.

a
Diptych, English, second quarter of the 14th century.
Silver gilt and translucent enamel.
On the left wing, the Resurrection and Ascension of Christ: on the right wing, the Coronation of the Virgin: below, Saints Christopher and George. Probably made for someone particularly devoted to St Christopher, patron of travellers, and to St George, patron of soldiers.
From the Spitzer and Salting collections.
h. 4.1 cm. w. 6.3 cm.
M.544-1910

b
Diptych, English or Flemish, 14th century.
Silver gilt and translucent enamel.
Left wing, the Resurrection: right wing, the Nativity: on the reverse are Ss. John the Baptist and Michael.
From the Webb collection.
h. 5 cm. w. 6.8 cm.
217-1874

c
The Campion Hall triptych, English, about 1350.
Gold and translucent enamel.
Above, the Coronation of the Virgin; left wing, St Christopher; right wing, All Saints; central panel, St Anne teaching the infant Virgin Mary to read, the Visitation (Elisabeth and the Virgin), St John the Baptist, St James of Compostella, St Edmund with his arrow of martyrdom, St Giles. Another enamel, a plaque of the Crucifixion, by the same goldsmith, is in the Metropolitan Museum, New York.
h. 7.2 cm. w. 8.1 cm.
On loan from Campion Hall, Oxford.

d
Triptych, English, mid-14th century.
Silver gilt with translucent enamel.
The Crucifixion with, on the left, the Holy Women at the Sepulchre, and below, the Harrowing of Hell; on the right are Christ appearing to Mary Magdalene and to Thomas. (The other side is shown in plate 32).
From the Salting collection.
h. 6.5 cm. w. 11.2 cm.
M.545-1910

e
Triptych, Flemish, 1325-50.
Silver gilt with translucent enamel.
On the left panel are the Annunciation and the Nativity; in the centre, the Adoration of the Magi; below, the Assumption of the Virgin and the Coronation of the Virgin; on the right are St Anne and the infant Virgin and Saints Catherine and Margaret.
h. 7.6 cm. w. 12.9 cm.
48-1867

32
Devotional altarpiece in the form of a triptych, English, mid-14th century.
Translucent enamel on silver gilt.
In the centre, the Resurrection; on the left, the Mocking and Scourging of Christ; on the right, the Descent from the Cross and Christ carrying the Cross. It is clear that the triptych has been wrongly assembled at some time, and that the centre panel should be reversed to allow the Crucifixion scene to appear on this side. The scenes would then read anti-clockwise, as is commonly found on contemporary ivories.

The engraving and range of colours used are exceptionally fine, yet they bear little resemblance to those of Parisian products, which are considered amongst the most skilful of the period. An English goldsmith may have made the piece, for there are resemblances between it and some East Anglican manuscripts, whilst the elaborately cusped borders of the side panel scenes are like those on the contemporary King's Lynn cup, which may have been made locally.
From the Salting collection.
w. 6.5 cm. h. 11.2 cm.
M.545-1910

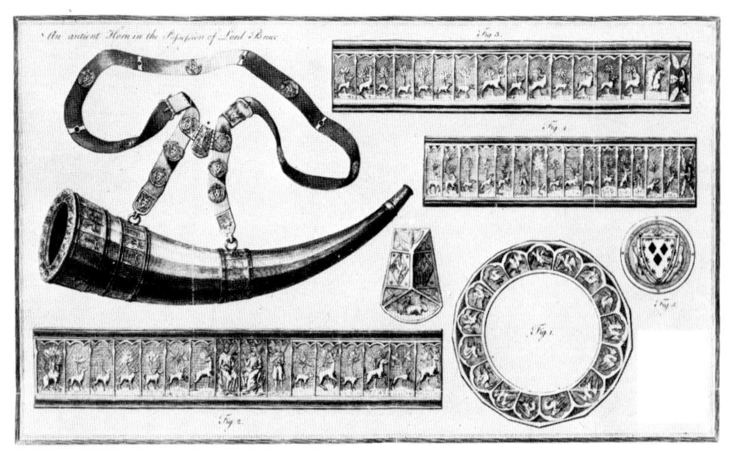

33
The Savernake Horn, English and Scottish, between 1314 and 1346.
An 18th century engraving showing the ivory horn mounted with bands of silver and translucent enamel, much of it missing. The leather baldric is mounted with 14 bosses of silver and champlevé enamel.
The uppermost band shows a king flanked by a bishop and a forester blowing a horn. The remaining compartments enclose hounds, stags, a unicorn, a hind, a hare, a fox and a lion, and on the lip are various birds. The second band shows similar animals and the third is an 18th century addition. Each of the baldric bosses is enamelled with arms, and the central boss depicts a lion, stag, butterfly and a bird.
The horn was, until its recent sale, the property of the Marquesses of Ailesbury, who inherited it in 1821 from the Seymour family, bailiffs and hereditary keepers of Savernake forest since the twelfth century. The horn appears in the 1604 pedigree of the Seymours, and it is thought that it was the symbol of their tenure of Savernake forest. However, the arms on the baldric are those of the Scottish Randolph family, created Earls of Moray about 1314 and extinct by 1346. There is no evidence of any contact between the families, suggesting that the baldric belonged originally to another horn, but was added to this one at some time before 1604. Both horn and baldric are, however, contemporary, and both were probably made in the British Isles.
One of the few other such ceremonial horns still in existence is at Maastricht, and is also mounted with formerly enamelled silver bands.
l. 66 cm.
The original horn is now in the British Museum.

34
The Presentation of the Magi, English, 15th century.
Gold with black champlevé enamel ground.
The plaque may have been part of a small reliquary. In technique and date it is very like both the unique Langdale rosary in the Museum, which is also decorated in black enamel with saints and scenes from the life of Christ, and with a number of gold rings enamelled with saints and Biblical subjects.
From the Joan Evans collection.
h. 3.5 cm. w. 2.8 cm.
M.51-1975

example of which is the Mérode cup [plate 36]. But encrusted enamel, first used towards the end of the fourteenth century, offered far greater scope, for it could be used both on small pieces of jewellery and to colour larger-scale sculptural works. A virtuoso example of the latter use is the splendid 'Goldenes Rössel' (little golden steed) group of 1403, now at Altötting [plate 37]; a comparable group in the British Museum is the Holy Thorn Reliquary of the Last Judgement, on which all twenty figures are enamelled.

35
Reichenau crozier, Constance, 1351.
Copper gilt, with plaques of silver and translucent enamel.
The Latin inscription indicates that the crozier was made for the abbot Master Eberhard of Brandis in 1351, through his treasurer Nicholas of Gutenberg. Eberhard, abbot of the island monastery of Reichenau on Lake Constance between 1343 and 1379, is probably the mitred figure kneeling to the Virgin and Child within the crook, while the figure of his treasurer, Nicholas, kneels beneath the supporting angel. The knop is set with enamelled plaques representing the Virgin and Child, the Three Magi, Mary Magdalen, and an abbot, perhaps St Pirmin, first abbot of Reichenau.
It is rare to find a piece of goldsmiths' work which bears a date. Its enamels are very similar to those on the chalice from St Johann zu Constanz of about 1320, now in the Walters Arts Gallery, Baltimore. Comparable croziers of a similar date, although probably of French origin, belong to Cologne Cathedral and to the Bishopric of Haarlem.
From the Soltikoff collection.
l. 31.7 cm. w. 12.7 cm.
7950-1862

In contrast to Northern European developments, goldsmiths in or near Venice appear to have rediscovered the techniques of filigree enamel. By the fifteenth century this was also being practised in Hungary, and some of the best surviving examples are Hungarian.

The earliest experiments with the new technique of painted enamel seem to have occurred in the Netherlands, where compositions in gold and white were painted on to a dark blue ground previously enamelled on gold or silver. Surviving pieces are very rare, although two are in the V &A collection [plates 1 & 38], while perhaps the most famous is the 'Monkey Cup' in the Metropolitan Museum, New York. In Venice, a form of painted enamel known as 'Turkish' was used to embellish domestic objects of copper, while elsewhere in Northern Italy painted enamel plaques on gold or silver were made to decorate ecclesiastical items. In France, a few scattered pieces—including a self-portrait medallion of about 1450 by Jean Fouquet—herald the rise, during the late fifteenth century, of the painted enamel workshops of Renaissance Limoges.

At this point, when a new iconography and a new technique eclipse the traditions of the past, the discussion of medieval enamels must end. Few of the objects mentioned above rank with master pieces such as the Chartres sculptures or the Ravenna mosaics, yet the historical interest of medieval enamels, and their considerable aesthetic appeal, have long assured them the devoted attention of both scholars and collectors.

36
The Mérode cup, Burgundian or French, early 15th century.
Silver-gilt decorated with pouncework and plique-a-jour enamel, the cells of gold.
The cup is unique and the earliest known example of plique-à-jour enamel. Such cups appear in the inventories of that great 14th-century patron of the arts, Jean, Duc de Berry, brother of King Charles V of France, and were very highly esteemed in their day.
Formerly owned by the Belgian family of Mérode and the collector Henry Bevan.
h. 17.5 cm. w. 9.3 cm.
403-1872

37
The 'Goldenes Rössel', French (Paris), about 1403.
Gold, with encrusted enamel; the base silver gilt.
The Virgin and Child, surrounded by Ss John the Baptist, John the Evangelist and Catherine, and King Charles VI of France, his squire, pageboy and horse. Given by Queen Isabel to her husband Charles VI as a new year's day present in 1404. This is one of the largest and most lavish of enamels 'en ronde bosse'.
h. 62 cm.
Altötting, Collegiate Church.

38
Plaque, Netherlandish, second quarter of the 15th century.
Painted enamel on gold.
Showing the Crucifixion, with the Virgin and St John the Evangelist. It may have been the centrepiece of a pax (the tablet kissed by the priest and people before taking Holy Communion). It is one of the earliest of the few survivors of this type of enamel, made for the wealthy Dukes of Burgundy and the French kings. Another painted enamel rare in showing a religious subject, that of the Virgin and Child, is a medallion in the Walters Art Gallery, Baltimore, which may have been made for Jean, Duc de Berry.
From the Magniac and Salting collections.
h. 4.1 cm. w. 2.6 cm.
M.546-1910

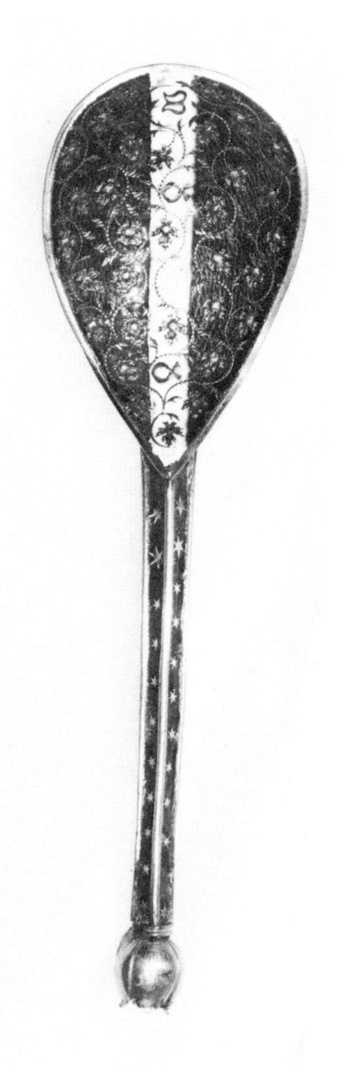

39
Spoon, possibly Venetian, late 15th century.
Silver gilt with translucent enamel.
An example of a sumptuous domestic object, embedded with silver stars and the repeated initials 'M' and 'O'. Similar spoons are in the Metropolitan Museum, New York, and the Kunsthistorisches Museum, Vienna.
From the Londesborough collection.
l. 17.4 cm.
1392-1888

The V&A Collection

Medieval enamels were amongst the earliest purchases in the 1850s of the newly founded museum. Interest in the subject was further stimulated by a large exhibition of enamels held here in 1874. Throughout the nineteenth century judicious purchases were made from the sales of such notable collectors as Bernal (1858), Prince Soltikoff (1861), Magniac (1892) and Frederick Spitzer (1893). The Museum has also profited from such generous bequests as those of George Salting (1910), W. L. Hildburgh (1956) and Joan Evans (1975).

The bulk of the collection had however, been acquired well before the second World War and includes some notable rarities. There can be no greater testimony to interest in the subject than the spur it provides to purveyors of the *ersatz*: a number of choice fake enamels in the medieval style were acquired as authentic by the Museum in the nineteenth century [see plate 40].

40
Devotional triptych, German, 19th century in the style of the 14th century.
Silver gilt set with plaques of translucent enamel on silver.
Representing Christ in Judgement, kneeling saints and angels holding instruments of the Passion; the base is set with precious stones. The enamels are copied from the Wolff-Metternich altarpiece in the Morgan Library, New York, and may have been made by Gabriel Hermeling of Cologne.
From the Webb collection.
h. 18.4 cm. w. 19.9 cm.
4684-1869

Further Reading

Medieval Enamels

These books discuss specific pieces and their techniques. To find the newest research, however, and to fill gaps in the available literature (particularly of the Gothic period), catalogues of recent medieval exhibitions must be consulted.

Chamot, Mary, *English Medieval Enamels*, London, 1930: still the only study of this subject, although not always adequately argued—the black and white illustrations are poor.

Dalton, O. M., *Catalogue of the Medieval Ivories, Enamels, Jewellery etc Bequeathed to the Fitzwilliam Museum by Frank McClean*, Cambridge, 1912: probably the best introduction to the subject yet available in English, although the comments on early Limoges work may be misleading in the light of more recent work—few illustrations.

De Laborde, M., *Notice des Emaux, Bijoux et Objets Divers du Musée du Louvre*, Paris, 1853: the introduction contains one of the earliest studies of the subject, and is still of interest.

Guth-Dreyfus, Katia, *Transluzides Email in der Ersten Hälfte des 14 Jahrhunderts am Ober-Mittel-und Niederrhein*, Basel, 1954: the most detailed discussion of translucent Gothic enamels, concentrating largely on those from the Rhineland—black and white illustrations.

Gauthier, M. M., *Les Emaux du Moyen Age*, Fribourg, 1972: the most comprehensive and up-to-date publication on the subject, if sometimes a little confusing. Lavishly illustrated in colour and black and white, with an excellent bibliography.

Hildburgh, W. L., *Medieval Spanish Enamels*, London, 1936: a well-argued and still contentious work which suggests that Spain was at least as prolific a centre of production as Limoges, and should be credited with many of its products—some black and white illustrations.

Rupin, E., *L'Oeuvre de Limoges*, Paris, 1890-2: the standard work on Limoges champlevé enamels, marred by a certain chauvinism—many illustrations in black and white.

Steingräber, E., 'Email' in *Reallexikon zur Deutschen Kunstgeschichte*, vol 5, Stuttgart, 1967: lucid and concise, the best recent history of the subject—extensive bibliography, but few illustrations.

Wessel, K., *Byzantine Enamels*, Shannon, 1969.

The Medieval Arts

These books discuss various types of enamels in the wider context of the architecture and sculpture, metalwork, painting, stained glass, textiles and dress of their period.

Evans, Joan, *A History of Jewellery 1100-1870*, 2nd ed., London, 1970: a good general survey of the subject, with full bibliography and black and white illustrations.

Focillon, H. (ed. Jean Bony), *The Art of the West* vol I *Romanesque* vol II *Gothic*, 3rd ed., Oxford, 1980: a comprehensive discussion of the stylistic evolution of medieval art, in an historical and philosophical context.

Hawthorne, John, Stanley Smith, Cyril, trans. & commentary, *Theophilus on Divers Arts*, 2nd ed., New York, 1979: a unique twelfth-century treatise on the techniques of painting, glass and metalwork translated and elucidated by a scholar and a metallurgist—full bibliography.

Henderson, George, *Gothic*, London, 1967: a useful general book, illustrated in colour and black and white.

Lasko, Peter, *Ars Sacra 800-1200 AD*, London, 1972: a comprehensive account of the form and decoration of church furnishings—whether of gold, silver, enamel, ivory or bronze—between the time of Charlemage and the beginning of the Gothic period—good black and white illustrations, extensive bibliography.

Lightbrown, R. W., *Secular Goldsmiths' Work in Medieval France: a History*, London, 1978: domestic plate of the Gothic period, with and without enamel, discussed in terms of its use, prestige and survival—black and white illustrations, extensive bibliography.

Oxford History of English Art series: all branches of the visual arts considered in chronological sequence, well illustrated in black and white, with copious bibliographies.

Panofsky, Erwin (ed. Panofsky-Soergel, G.), *Abbot Suger on the Abbey Church of St Denis and its Art Treasures*, 2nd ed., Princeton, 1979:
a translation of, and commentary upon, the influential writings of this twelfth-century abbot.

Steingräber, Eric, *Antique Jewellery: its History in Europe 800–1900*, London, 1970:
a good survey of the subject, particularly valuable for its coverage of the early medieval period—full bibliography, colour and black and white illustrations.

Swarzenski, Hanns, *Monuments of Romanesque Art*, 2nd ed., London, 1974:
a very brief introduction precedes a concise catalogue of ecclesiastical objects in all media, fully illustrated in black and white.

Theophilus: see *Hawthorne*

Zarnecki, George, *Romanesque Art*, London, 1971:
a selective but lucid discussion well illustrated in colour and black and white.

Exhibitions

Athens, 1964 *Byzantine Art*

Brussels and Cologne, 1972 *Rhein und Maas, Kunst und Kultur* 800–1400

Cologne, 1978 *Die Parler und der Schone Stil 1350–1400*

London, 1976 *Jewellery Through 7000 Years*

Ottawa, 1972 *Art and the Courts (France and England from 1259–1328)*

Paris, 1965 *Les Trésors des Eglises de France*

Paris, 1968 *L'Europe Gothique XII–XIV Siècles*

Paris, 1981 *Les Fastes du Gothique: le Siècle de Charles V*

Stuttgart, 1977 *Die Ziet der Staufer*

Vienna, 1962 *Europaische Kunst um 1400*